FANTASTIC FACTS ABOUT

STARS & PLANETS

Author
Tim Furniss

Editor
Steve Parker

Design
Pentacor

Image Co-ordination
Ian Paulyn

Production Assistant
Rachel Jones

Index
Jane Parker

Editorial Director
Paula Borton

Design Director
Clare Sleven

Publishing Director
Jim Miles

This is a Parragon Book
First published in 2000

Parragon, Queen Street House, 4 Queen Street, Bath, BA1 1HE, UK

Copyright © Parragon 2000

Parragon has previously printed this material in 1999 as part of the Factfinder series

2 4 6 8 10 9 7 5 3 1

Produced by Miles Kelly Publishing Ltd
Bardfield Centre, Great Bardfield, Essex CM7 4SL

ISBN 0-75253-385-1

Printed in Italy Milanostampa Caleppio Milano

FANTASTIC FACTS ABOUT

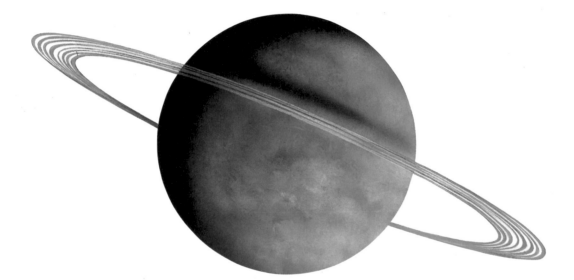

STARS & PLANETS

p

CONTENTS

INTRODUCTION

There are few subjects more interesting than the night sky, with its constellations of stars and planets. Earth is the only planet where life is known to exist, and the Sun is merely a medium-sized star among millions in the Milky Way Galaxy. Now, thanks to modern technology, we are just beginning to understand some of the mysteries of the ever-expanding Universe.

STARS AND PLANETS is a handy reference guide in the *Fascinating Facts* series. Each book has been specially compiled with a collection of stunning illustrations and photographs which bring the subject to life. Hundreds of facts and figures are presented in a variety of interesting ways and fact-panels which provide information at-a-glance. This unique combination is fun and easy to use and makes learning a pleasure.

OUR EARTH

Ever since the first humans peered in wonder at the stars in the night sky, we have longed to know more about the Universe. Today, we have the technology to explore deeper into the Universe than ever imagined. The Earth is just one very tiny part of the vast Universe – a small rocky planet travelling around a medium-sized star, the Sun, in one of billions of galaxies. Nobody really knows where the Universe begins or ends. Even though the most powerful radio telescope has detected a quasar 13,200 million light-years away, we have so far explored only a very small part of the Universe.

THE EARTH AND ITS MOON
This is a view of the Earth as seen from another world in space – from our neighbour, the Moon. This classic photograph of the space age was taken by the crew of Apollo *8 in December 1968.*

THE NIGHT SKY

For around 400 years, most of our knowledge about the night sky and 'what is out there' came from light telescopes. There are two main kinds: refracting telescopes that use only lenses (far left), and reflecting telescopes that use mirrors and lenses (near left). From the 1930s, radio telescopes were able to detect other rays and waves from space.

FARTHER THAN EVER

Scientists believe that the Universe is expanding all the time. Groups of galaxies are rushing away from our Milky Way Galaxy, and also from each other. As a result, the distances between galaxies are increasing, and the Universe is getting bigger and bigger. The stars within these galaxies are slowly changing too, and new ones are constantly forming. The huge columns of cool interstellar gas and dust known as nebulae are the birthplaces of new stars. The Eagle Nebula, also known as M16, is in the constellation Serpens in the northern sky. Its tallest pillar is one light-year long, and our whole Solar System could be swallowed up inside one of the 'fingertips' at the top of the column.

PLANETS AND MOONS
A montage of images taken by NASA's Voyager 1 *and* 2 *spacecraft shows the beautiful ringed planet Saturn and a few of its many moons.*

DISTANT NEBULA
This awe-inspiring image from the
Hubble Space Telescope shows the
Eagle Nebula, which is 7,000 light-
years away from the Earth.

THE UNIVERSE

The Universe is everything that exists. It stretches farther almost than the human mind can imagine – we already know that the Universe reaches at over 13 billion light-years in every direction. The Universe is filled with matter in many different shapes, sizes and forms. It contains dust and gases; planets such as the Earth and Jupiter; the Sun and billions of other stars; our Milky Way Galaxy and countless galaxies.

Our tiny planet Earth has a unique place in the Universe because it is the only place where we know that life definitely exists. There is still so much for us to discover about the vast Universe – about how it began and where it might end. One day we might even discover life in other parts of our Universe, or even the existence of other universes.

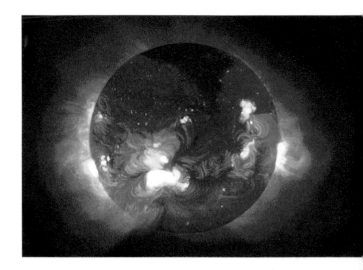

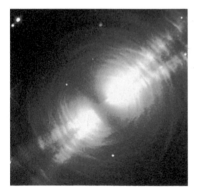

HOME IN THE COSMOS

 We can begin to understand the size of the Universe, and our place in it, by writing an address such as this: Jane Smith, Human Being, 5 Robins Avenue, Raleigh, Newtown, Yorkshire, England, United Kingdom, Europe, The Earth, The Solar System, The Milky Way, Galaxy Group C7, The Universe. The Earth is one of nine planets that move round the Sun, forming what we call the Solar System. The Sun is just one of over 100,000 million stars in a galaxy which we call the Milky Way. The Milky Way is just one of millions of other galaxies in the vast Universe.

The Earth is a unique part of the Universe since it is the only place where we know that life definitely exists. This life is not just small microbes but a life of incredible variety. About 5,000 million human beings live on Earth, yet we are just one kind of being among over 1 million different species.

THE BEGINNING OF TIME

The powerful Hubble Space Telescope is able to look back into the 'beginning of time'. This image reveals a small number of the countless multi-coloured galaxies of all shapes and sizes that are found in the Universe.

HORSEHEAD NEBULA

The Horsehead Nebula is a cloud of cool dust. Here it is seen rising up against a backdrop of hot gas. The gas is glowing with energy from nearby stars.

THE VAST UNIVERSE

The image (above left) from the Hubble Space Telescope shows a part of our night sky. It covers an area that is just 1/30th the size of the Moon as we see it in the sky. Some of the galaxies are so far away that they are up to four billion times fainter than the limits of human vision. Although this image covers a very small area of the sky, it shows a typical arrangement of galaxies in space. In fact, from a statistical point of view the Universe looks the same in every direction.

SUN AND SOLAR SYSTEM

The Sun is a very ordinary star among thousands of millions of other stars in the Milky Way Galaxy. It has a planetary system, called the Solar System, which is made up of planets and other 'left-over' material that did not form into planets. The nine known planets start with Mercury, which is at an average distance of 57.9 million kilometres from the Sun. Then comes Venus, the Earth, Mars, Jupiter, Saturn, Uranus, Neptune and Pluto. Between the orbits of Mars and Jupiter lies an area of one kind of left-over material, the asteroids. These are lumps of

Earth

Venus

Mars

Mercury

Jupiter   Saturn   Neptune   Uranus

Earth   Mars   Pluto

Venus   Mercury

THE PLANETS OF THE SOLAR SYSTEM
This montage shows all the planets of the Solar System, compared in size. Mercury, the planet nearest to the Sun, is on the left, and Earth is third from the left. Jupiter is the largest planet. Pluto, the ninth and last planet, is almost too small to see.

rock, some of which are many kilometres long. Beyond Pluto is another kind of left-over material, the comets. These are bodies of rock, ice and dust. When some comets pass close to the Sun they heat up and give off material, forming a tail. Comets also give off small rocky particles which form many of the meteors, or 'shooting stars', that we see.

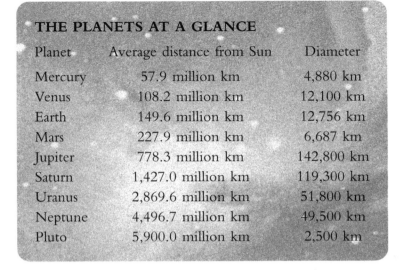

THE PLANETS AT A GLANCE

Planet	Average distance from Sun	Diameter
Mercury	57.9 million km	4,880 km
Venus	108.2 million km	12,100 km
Earth	149.6 million km	12,756 km
Mars	227.9 million km	6,687 km
Jupiter	778.3 million km	142,800 km
Saturn	1,427.0 million km	119,300 km
Uranus	2,869.6 million km	51,800 km
Neptune	4,496.7 million km	49,500 km
Pluto	5,900.0 million km	2,500 km

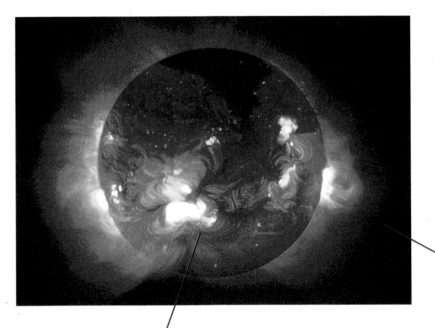

SUPER-HOT SUN
If we had X-ray eyes, this is how the Sun would look to us. This image shows the Sun's turbulent atmosphere. In the outer layer, or corona, temperatures reach as high as 2 million degrees Celsius.

The corona is the outer layer of the Sun's atmosphere

The photosphere, or surface, of the Sun

THE SPEED OF LIGHT

As we know, our Earth is a very small but rather important part of the vast Universe. The Universe is so huge that we cannot measure it in kilometres, or even millions of kilometres. Imagine writing down in kilometres the distance of the Andromeda Galaxy from Earth. It would take millions of numbers – far too many to fit on a page of this book. So astronomers measure the size of the Universe or the distance of stars by using the speed at which light from these objects travels. Light travels in empty space at a speed of 299,792.456 kilometres per second. (It travels a little slower when passing through water, glass or other denser media.) The distance that light travels in one year – 9.46 million million kilometres – is called a light-year.

Light from the Sun, which is about 150 million kilometres from Earth, takes 8 minutes to reach us. The nearest star, Proxima Centauri, is 4.225 light-years from Earth.

LIGHT ON THE MOVE
Light from the most distant galaxy so far detected in the Universe took 13,100 billion years to reach the Earth. Light from the Sun takes just 8 minutes!

THE MILKY WAY
These are some of the stars in our Milky Way Galaxy. The brightest star in our night sky is also one of the nearest. It is called Sirius, in the constellation Canis Major, and is 8.6 light-years away from Earth.

THE ANDROMEDA GALAXY
The nearest galaxy to our Milky Way Galaxy is the spectacular Andromeda Galaxy. It can just be seen with the naked eye as a small fuzzy patch of light in the northern skies, near the constellation Pegasus.

THE MILKY WAY

THE MILKY WAY GALAXY
No one knows exactly what the Milky Way
Galaxy looks like from the outside. It is a
spiral-shaped galaxy, with arms that resemble
the shape of a spinning firework.

We can see about 5,000 individual stars in the night sky. On a really clear night, it is also possible to see one or two galaxies. The most visible part of our own Milky Way Galaxy is the part of the sky that looks like a misty cloud. It is really a band of millions of stars. This part of our Galaxy that we can actually see is also called the Milky Way. When we look at it, we are looking towards the centre of our Galaxy where there are the most stars. We cannot actually see the centre because we are situated a long way from the centre in the Orion arm, an outer arm of the Galaxy. When we look at the region where the famous Orion constellation is situated, there seem to be fewer stars. This is because we are looking towards the edge of the Galaxy.

Halley's Comet

HALLEY'S COMET
This photo of the Milky Way also shows Halley's Comet passing across the sky. A comet orbits the Sun, and so it is much closer to Earth than the distant stars.

OUR GALAXY
If we could look at it from the side, the Milky Way Galaxy would be a rather thin disc with a dense, bulging centre surrounded by a halo. This halo is a mass of older stars surrounding the central mass, which contains the most stars. The thinner edges of the disc are the outer arms of the Galaxy. The Milky Way Galaxy is about 2,000 light-years thick but 100,000 light-years across. It contains an estimated 100,000 million stars. Our Sun, which is one of those stars, is about 30,000 light-years from the centre. It orbits the centre of the Galaxy at a speed of 274 kilometres per second.

BIRTH OF THE STARS
In addition to the millions of stars in the Milky Way Galaxy, there are also many nebulae, which are regions where stars are being born. This is a nebula in the constellation Cygnus.

21

GALAXIES AND NEBULAE

When we look into the night sky, we can observe other objects in addition to stars. Some, like nebulae, are inside the Milky Way, while others are distant galaxies much farther away. The most famous nebula is part of the constellation Orion (the Hunter). Hanging from the hunter's 'belt' of three stars is a 'sword' of stars. In the middle of the sword is the Orion Nebula, a region of hot gas and dust where new stars are born. The nebula is 1,500 light-years away and 15 light-years across.

The most famous galaxy is the Andromeda Galaxy, which is close to the constellation Pegasus. It is the most distant object visible to the naked eye and looks like a small

Central band of dust and cloud

SOMBRERO GALAXY
This is a spectacular, almost perfectly formed galaxy called the Sombrero Galaxy. It is also called a nebula because it has a prominent central band of dust and cloud.

fuzzy patch. The Andromeda Galaxy is a huge spiral galaxy, 2.2 billion light-years away. It is thought to contain at least 300 billion stars.

DYING STARS

Some nebulae are the remnants of dying stars. The mysterious 'searchlight' beams emerging from a hidden star in the Egg Nebula (left) are being criss-crossed by many bright arcs. The nebula is a huge cloud of dust and gas ejected by a dying star. The star, which is hidden by a dense cocoon of dust, is expanding at a speed of 20 kilometres per second. Eventually the dying star will blow off its outer layers to form a planetary nebula.

The Egg Nebula is a swirling cloud of gas and dust

EGG NEBULA

This strange-looking nebula, called the Egg Nebula, is 3,000 light-years away from Earth. This photo was taken by the Hubble Space Telescope, which has helped to revolutionize astronomy.

THE VAST UNIVERSE

Scientists estimate that there are billions of galaxies in the Universe, but we cannot be sure because no one knows where the Universe ends – if it does! People who believe that the Universe was created by a god or gods can accept that it is beyond our human understanding. There are also many people who believe that the Universe was not created but just 'happened', perhaps in a 'big bang'; its glory was simply an accident. Whatever people think, the human race will perhaps never fully understand the nature of the Universe. However, this lack of understanding will not stop us trying

SPACE AND TIME

Space is not straight, continuous or constant. Neither is time. In the relationship between space and time, space curves around massive objects, such as stars, while time speeds up or slows down. The Universe is filled with mysterious objects such as black holes, and perhaps even 'short-cuts', or wormholes, to other dimensions or even other universes.

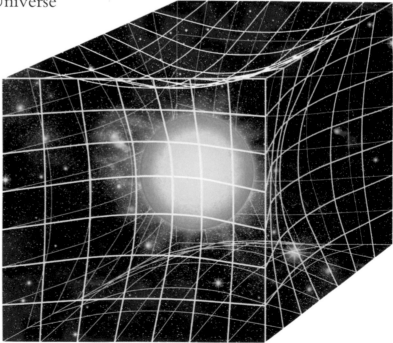

to find out more about the Universe, through observation and exploration. Yet each new and exciting discovery seems to create even more questions to be answered!

THE VAST UNIVERSE
We may only be able to see a very small section of a much larger Universe. The size of the Universe is so great that human beings can only begin to perceive it.

BIGGER AND FARTHER

In 1990, astronomers discovered a galaxy called Abell 2029 in the constellation Virgo. The Abell 2029 Galaxy is 1,070 million light-years away and has an incredible diameter of 5.6 million light-years, which is 80 times bigger than the Milky Way. The most remote object yet discovered in the Universe is over 13 million light-years away and is a quasar inside a galaxy. Quasars are mysterious space objects which are thought to be associated with equally mysterious black holes.

EVERYTHING THAT EXISTS
The Universe contains everything that exists. It contains all of space, time and matter. There could be millions of other galaxies like our Milky Way in the Universe. The most distant galaxy that we have detected so far is over 13 million light-years away.

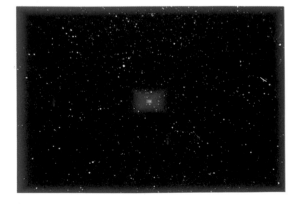

25

SIGNPOSTS IN THE SKY

 Long ago, people divided up the night sky into distinct areas called constellations. The word 'constellation' also refers to a pattern of stars that appears in a particular area of the sky. Many of these star patterns are named after animals or figures from mythology.

Astronomers have named a total of 88 different constellations. The most famous one in the night sky of the northern hemisphere is probably Ursa Major, or the Great Bear. It contains a well-known group of stars called the Plough. Even people who are not interested in astronomy can usually locate the Plough easily. It is sometimes described as being like a saucepan with a bent handle. It has four main stars which form an outline rather like that of a saucepan. The bent handle consists of another three main stars.

Polaris, or Pole Star

The Plough

THE PLOUGH

The Plough makes a wonderful signpost in the sky. The two upright stars on the right-hand side of the saucepan point up to a star called Polaris. This is the Pole Star, the nearest star to the place in the northern skies to which the Earth's axis points. Because the Earth rotates on its own axis, the Pole Star looks as if it remains in the same place in the sky as the other stars move around it.

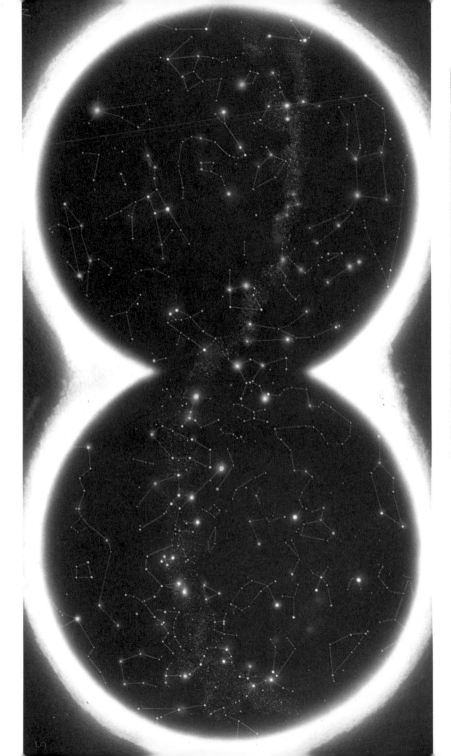

ORION AND PEGASUS

The magnificent constellation Orion dominates the winter sky in the northern hemisphere. Not only can it be used as a signpost, but it is also one of the constellations that really seems to look like the character it depicts – the Hunter. We can clearly make out his belt and sword, and to the right his bent bow and arrow pointing at the horns of an angry bull – Taurus. The Orion Nebula is visible within the third star of the Hunter's sword. The famous Andromeda Galaxy can be located using the almost perfect 'square' set of stars in the constellation Pegasus.

THE NIGHT SKIES
This map shows the stars and constellations of the northern (top) and southern (bottom) hemispheres. The sky in the northern hemisphere is shown as it appears from the North Pole. Polaris, the Pole Star, is directly overhead. There is no equivalent of the Pole Star in the southern hemisphere.

BRIGHTEST STARS

 The measure of a star's brightness is called its magnitude. The smaller the magnitude, the brighter the star is. The first person to work out a level of brightness was probably a Greek astronomer called Hipparchus. He divided the stars as he could see them into six groups. The stars in the brightest group were first magnitude, and the faintest stars were sixth magnitude. Later, other astronomers worked out that Hipparchus's brightest stars were about 100 times brighter than sixth-magnitude stars. The stars that were 100 times brighter than sixth magnitude were given a minus number, and the fainter ones were given a plus number. One of the brightest stars, Arcturus, the main star of the constellation Boötes, has a magnitude of –0.06.

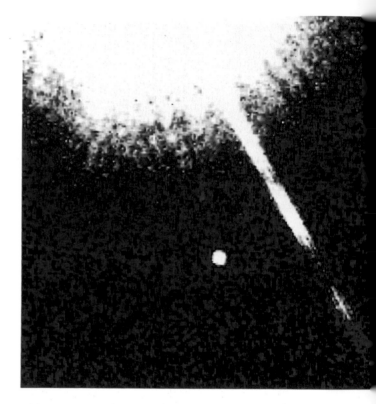

STAR BRIGHT
This dramatic picture shows a high-resolution image of a star. Out of the 14 brightest stars in the night sky, 11 of them are visible in the northern hemisphere.

WITH THE NAKED EYE

We can see about 5,000 stars in the night sky with the naked eye. Fainter stars can be seen only with binoculars or telescopes.

THE 14 BRIGHTEST STARS

Star	Constellation	Magnitude
Sirius	Canis Major	−1.45
Canopus	Carina	−0.73
Alpha Centauri	Centaurus	−0.1
Arcturus	Boötes	−0.06
Vega	Lyra	−0.04
Capella	Auriga	−0.08
Rigel	Orion	−0.11
Procyon	Canis Minor	+0.35
Achernar	Eridanus	+0.48
Beta Centauri	Centaurus	+0.6
Altair	Aquila	+0.77
Betelgeuse	Orion	+0.8
Aldebaran	Taurus	+0.85
Acrux	Crux	+0.09

Betelgeuse

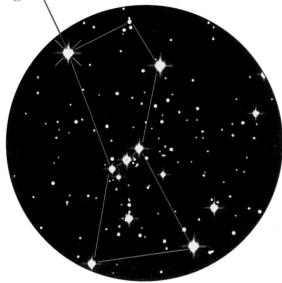

BETELGEUSE

Betelgeuse, in the constellation Orion, is an old and dying red giant star. This picture was taken by the Hubble Space Telescope. Betelgeuse is about 310 light-years away from Earth. It has a diameter of about 500 million kilometres and could swallow up the Solar System almost as far as the planet Jupiter.

29

MOVING STARS

The Earth's spinning motion makes the stars seem to move across the night sky. The exception is the Pole Star, which seems to stay in the same place with the other stars revolving around it. The southern night sky has no Pole Star, and the area in the sky to which the Earth's South Pole points is almost empty of bright stars. The long axis of the famous Southern Cross (Crux) constellation in the southern sky points to the south celestial pole, the sky's south pole.

You are probably used to seeing a constellation, such as Orion, in the northern night sky. If you move closer to the Equator you will see the constellation on its side. As you move south, it will appear upside down and eventually disappear the farther south you travel. The same phenomena will happen to the southern stars as you travel north. The farther south you travel, the more of the southern sky you will see and the less of the north.

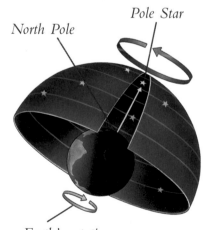

North Pole

Pole Star

Earth's rotation

Pole Star

AT THE NORTH POLE
If you stood on the North Pole and looked up at the night sky, the Pole Star would be directly above your head. Because the Earth's axis points almost directly to the Pole Star, the other stars seem to revolve around it as the Earth rotates.

NORTH OF THE EQUATOR

If you stand on the Earth somewhere between 10 and 20 degrees north of the Equator, you will be in the mid-northern latitudes. The stars overhead will still seem to be moving, slowly changing the appearance of the sky from night to night.

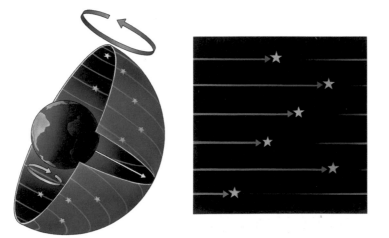

AT THE EQUATOR

An observer who stands at the Equator will see all the stars in the night sky during the period of a year. At the Equator, the stars seem to move in straight lines across the sky.

THE SOLAR SYSTEM

The Sun, together with the family of nine planets, comets, asteroids and other bodies that travel round it, make up our Solar System. It was probably formed from a cloud of gas around 4.6 billion years ago. At the very heart of the Solar System lies the Sun, providing the heat and light that make life possible on the planet Earth.

Spacecraft have visited all of the planets, with the exception of Pluto, the smallest and most distant planet. They have revealed a wealth of

different features on the planets,
including mountains and valleys, craters
and active volcanoes, coloured ring systems,
poisonous atmospheres and polar ice-caps.
Earth is still the only planet in the Solar
System where we know that life definitely
exists, although scientists are continuously
looking for signs of life on all of the other
planets.

THE SUN AND FAMILY

Scientists believe that the Sun was born out of a cloud of hot gas and dust. As it started to become a fully fledged star, the remaining material was left orbiting the Sun at high speed. Specks of dust began to join together and form tiny rocks, which fused together gradually forming large bodies surrounded by clouds of gas. These bodies are the planets. The Solar System consists of nine known major planets: Mercury, Venus, Earth, Mars, Jupiter, Saturn, Uranus, Neptune and Pluto.

Other material was left orbiting the Sun when the Solar System was formed. It includes the asteroids, a network of smaller minor planets most of which are orbiting the Sun between Mars and Jupiter. Other left-over material includes comets and small and large pieces of rock, called meteoroids, which travel in random orbits around the Sun.

THE EARTH IS FORMED
The Sun was formed out of a spinning cloud of gas and dust. The rest of the Solar System is thought to be made up of the remaining material left over after the formation of the Sun. The gas and dust attracted other material which slowly developed into the planets, including the Earth.

SATURN , THE RINGED PLANET
*The planet Saturn is considered to be the 'star' of the Solar
System. It has a well-formed system of rings and a number of
moons. The other outer planets have much smaller ring systems.*

THE GAS PLANETS

Saturn is one of the four large gaseous planets in the Solar System. The others are Jupiter, Uranus and Neptune. These large planets, which have small solid cores, are made mainly of frozen gas. Saturn's rings may consist of the original material left over when the Solar System was formed. Another, more likely theory is that the rings are the remains of a moon that came too close and then disintegrated under the forces of the planet's gravity. Jupiter, one of the other gas planets, is so large and has such a huge atmosphere that many astronomers believe it almost became a star.

HALLEY'S COMET
*Comets are made of material left
over when the planets were formed.
They consist of dust and frozen
gases. Comets shine in the sky
because they are lit up by the
Sun as they pass close to it.*

THE SUN

 The Sun is 150 million kilometres away from the Earth. Its diameter at the equator is 1,392,000 kilometres. The Sun is 109 times the size of the Earth and contains 99.9 percent of the mass of the whole Solar System. The Sun's centre is like a huge nuclear furnace in which the temperature and pressure inside are so high that they set off atomic reactions. Here, atoms of hydrogen fuse together to form helium, and the energy produced at the core radiates out towards the surface.

The surface of the Sun is called the photosphere. The temperature here ranges from 4,300 degrees Celsius to 9,000 degrees Celsius. The photosphere provides most of the light that comes from the Sun. The upper level of the photosphere, the chromosphere, is a stormy region of very hot gases. Here, the temperature has risen to 1 million degrees Celsius. The chromosphere is about 16,000 kilometres thick. Above it, the Sun has a halo of even hotter gases called the corona.

SOLAR ACTIVITY
Bright arches of hot glowing gas erupt from the surface of the Sun. These arches are called prominences. They may reach as far as 30 kilometres above the Sun's surface. Some have a loop shape (above), while others are like a curtain of gas.

Helium core

Hydrogen layer

Solar flare

Photosphere

Chromosphere

Sunspot

THE SOLAR WIND

The outer layers of the corona are made up of hot gases blowing off from the Sun. This stream of gases is called the solar wind. It flows away from the Sun and through the Solar System. Sometimes, when the solar wind meets up with the Earth's upper atmosphere, or ionosphere, it causes magnetic storms and radio interference. The solar wind also causes auroras, the red and green glowing lights that are visible in the night sky in the extreme parts of the northern and southern hemispheres.

OUR NEAREST STAR

The Sun is the nearest star to the Earth. It is a main-sequence yellow dwarf star and is rather insignificant compared with the much larger stars in the Milky Way. Light from the Sun takes 8 minutes 17 seconds to reach the Earth, compared with the 4.3 light-years it takes to come from the next nearest star, Proxima Centauri. The centre of the Sun is a huge nuclear furnace with a temperature of 15 million degrees Celsius.

MERCURY

Mercury, the nearest planet to the Sun, is a small rocky body with a diameter of 4,880 kilometres. The planet takes just 88 Earth days to travel once around the Sun at a distance of between 69 million kilometres and just 49 million kilometres. the average distance of Mercury from the Sun is 57 million kilometres, which is about half as close to the Sun as the Earth is.

The Sun sometimes appears twice as large in the sky above Mercury.

The temperature in the intense sunlight on Mercury is 420 degrees Celsius, which is hot enough to melt lead at midday. Mercury rotates very slowly, once every 58 Earth days. Because of this, each day on Mercury lasts 176 Earth days. The night-time temperature is −180 degrees Celsius. There is no atmosphere on Mercury and it would be impossible to live there.

MERCURY IN VIEW
Nobody knew what Mercury looked like until a space probe flew past the planet and took close-up pictures. Mercury looks very like our own Moon. Its surface is covered with craters and mountains.

MERCURY FACT FILE

Diameter: 4,880 km

Average distance from Sun: 57.9 million km

Length of a year: 88 Earth days

Number of moons: 0

A HOT, DRY PLANET

Mercury is a very hot, dry and airless place. The planet is surrounded by a very thin layer of gases. Its surface is covered with many craters, which were probably formed when meteorites or comets crashed into the planet.

VENUS

Venus is surrounded by thick clouds of carbon dioxide gas. These clouds, which trap the Sun's heat and prevent it from escaping, help to create a greenhouse effect on the planet. The trapped heat raises the temperature on the surface to 475 degrees Celsius, despite only about 2 percent of the Sun's light reaching the surface. The atmospheric pressure on Venus is 90 times greater than on Earth. Also, it rains sulphuric acid there. So if you stood on Venus, you would be boiled, squashed and dissolved in one go! Venus is almost the same size as the Earth, measuring 12,100 kilometres in diameter. It orbits the Sun at a distance of 108 million kilometres and takes 224 days to make one orbit, during which it sometimes comes within 40 million kilometres of the Earth. Because Venus rotates once every 243 days, a Venus day lasts 116 Earth days. Its thick clouds reflect the sunlight, making it one of the brightest objects in the sky.

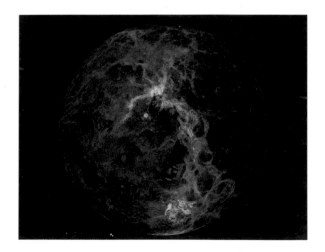

EARTH'S 'TWIN' PLANET
Venus is almost the same size as the Earth. It used to be known as Earth's sister or twin until people realized what was hidden beneath its thick sulphuric clouds. The surface of the planet is very hot and dry.

Before the surface of Venus could be seen in telescopes, and before spacecraft went close to it, Venus was seen as a rather romantic world. It was viewed as lying beneath a veil of clouds that reached a height of about 100 kilometres above the surface. People assumed that Venus, like Earth, had water. Because the planet is closer to the Sun than we are, many people, even in the 1960s, thought that the planet's surface was like a tropical jungle.

BRIGHT PLANET

The thick clouds that make up Venus's atmosphere reflect the sunlight brightly. It is therefore the brightest object in the Earth's skies apart from the Sun and the Moon. The planet's surface is covered with mountains, craters and volcanoes, some of them bigger than Mount Everest, the highest mountain on the Earth.

VENUS FACT FILE

Diameter: 12,100 km

Average distance from Sun: 108.2 million km

Length of a year: 225 Earth days

Number of moons: 0

41

THE EARTH

The Earth orbits the Sun, at an average distance of 150 million kilometres, once every 365 days, or year. As it orbits the Sun, the Earth is rotating at a speed of 1,660 kilometres per hour. It makes one rotation every 24 hours, or day. The Earth travels through space at a speed of almost 30 kilometres per second, and in a year it travels a total distance of 960 million kilometres.

The Earth has one moon which orbits at an average distance of 384,400 kilometres.

The Earth has an atmosphere that is rich in oxygen (21 percent) and nitrogen (78 percent). This atmosphere protects the Earth from deadly radiation from the Sun. About 70 percent of the Earth's surface is covered in liquid water in the form of the seas and oceans.

THE EARTH FROM SPACE
When seen from space, the Earth is the most beautiful and brightest planet. About three-quarters of its surface are covered by very reflective oceans of water. If we could see the Earth from another planet, it would look like a bright bluish star.

SPACESHIP EARTH

The Earth is like a spaceship. It travels through space at a speed of almost 30 kilometres per second, covering a distance of 960 million kilometres in a year. Although the Earth has a diameter of 12,756 kilometres, it has a very thin crust which is only 32 kilometres thick.

EARTH FACT FILE

Diameter: 12,756 km

Average distance from Sun: 150 million km

Length of a year: 365.25 Earth days

Number of moons: 1

43

OUR MOON

The Moon is about one-third the size of the Earth and has a diameter of 3,476 kilometres in diameter. The Moon–Earth system is sometimes referred to as a 'double planet'. The Moon orbits the Earth every 27.5 days, travelling at a speed of 3,700 kilometres per hour. Its surface is very dark because only about 7 percent of the Sun's light is reflected by it. The temperature on the Moon varies from 105 degrees Celsius in the bright sunlight to minus –155 degrees Celsius in the shade.

The pull of gravity on the Moon is only one-sixth of that on the Earth. When you look at the Moon you can see the famous 'Man in the Moon' face. This 'face' is created by the lighter areas on the Moon's surface, which are covered by craters and mountains, and by the darker areas which are flat, wide plains. These

PHASES OF THE MOON
When the Moon is between the Sun and the Earth its far side is lit up, so we cannot see the side that faces us. When the Moon has moved farther round in its orbit we can see a crescent shape (far left), which gets bigger until a full Moon (centre) appears.

plains were mistaken for 'seas' by early astronomers, which explains why they have such names as Sea of Tranquillity.

INSIDE THE MOON
Scientists believe that the Moon's outer layer, or crust, is between 60 and 100 kilometres thick. Beneath the crust is a thick layer of rock. The Moon's core is partly solid and partly liquid.

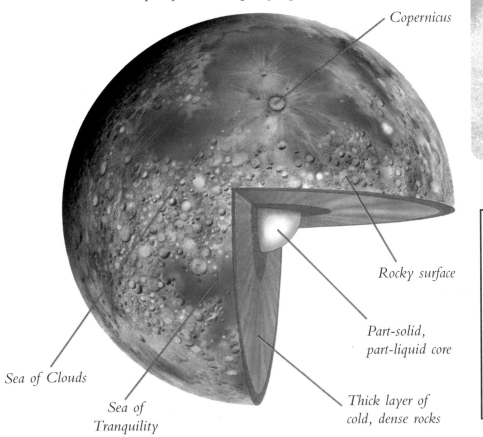

Copernicus

Rocky surface

Part-solid, part-liquid core

Sea of Clouds

Sea of Tranquility

Thick layer of cold, dense rocks

MOON FACT FILE

Diameter: 3,476 km

Average distance from Earth: 384,400 km

Time taken to make a complete orbit of Earth: 27.5 Earth days

Average speed of orbit: 3,700 km/h

MARS

Mars has always excited astronomers because it is the only planet that can be observed clearly from Earth using quite small telescopes. Mars has a diameter of 6,787 kilometres and orbits the Sun every 687 days – the length of a Martian year. The length of a day on Mars is similar to that on Earth – 24 hours and 37 minutes.

Unlike the Earth, the atmosphere on Mars is 95 percent carbon dioxide. A maximum Martian temperature of −29 degrees Celsius makes Mars as cold as the coldest place on Earth. The atmospheric pressure there is just 1 percent that of the Earth's, so Mars would not be able to support life as we know it. Mars has two moons called Deimos and Phobos. They are huge chunks of rock shaped like pockmarked potatoes. Phobos, the largest and closest one, is 27 kilometres long and 19 kilometres wide.

VIKING VISIT TO MARS

This image of the surface of Mars was taken by a Viking spacecraft which landed on the planet in 1976. The Martian surface is covered with reddish sand, dotted with various different sizes of rocks. The sand looks as though it may have been deposited by running water, which has also smoothed the rocks.

Early observations by telescope showed the dark areas on Mars changing shape during the year. The planet's polar ice-caps were also sighted. People then started to think that water from the melting ice-caps was helping to cultivate large areas of vegetation during the summer. One astronomer thought he could see lines on Mars, and the idea took off that there were Martians who had built irrigation canals! Mars then became the subject of many 'sci-fi' stories, such as the famous H.G.Wells story *War of the Worlds*.

THE RED PLANET

Mars is sometimes called the Red Planet because it has a reddish surface, which indicates the presence of iron oxide in the soil. On the Earth, iron oxide is known as rust. Mars has a very active environment with dust storms, fog, frost and polar ice-caps made of dry carbon dioxide and water ice. Mars has a spectacular landscape of volcanoes, craters and canyons.

MARS FACT FILE

Diameter: 6,787 km

Average distance from Sun: 227.9 million km

Length of a year: 687 Earth days

Number of moons: 2

ASTEROIDS

When the Solar System was formed,
large rocks were left orbiting the Sun.
Many of these rocks collided with each
other, causing more fragments. These
fragments are known as minor planets,
or asteroids. There could be 50,000
asteroids orbiting the Sun, about
2,500 of which are known to
be in a belt between the orbits
of Mars and Jupiter. The first
asteroid to be discovered –
and, not surprisingly,
the biggest – is called
Ceres. The brightest
asteroid, Vesta, is
just visible with
the naked eye.

There are other asteroids in elliptical orbits around the Sun. These come close to the Earth in their orbits, then travel far out into the deepest parts of the Solar System. They are called 'Sun-grazers'. It is quite possible that asteroids have hit the Earth, causing extensive damage to its surface and the atmosphere. An asteroid impact might have been the cause of an explosion in 1908 in Siberia. It had a force equivalent to that of a 13-megaton nuclear bomb.

ROCKY BODIES

Many thousands of asteroids orbit the Sun. These rocky bodies are the bits and pieces of material which seem to have been left over when the Solar System was formed. Although the largest asteroid is almost 1,000 kilometres wide, most of the known asteroids are less than 20 kilometres in diameter.

'SUN-GRAZERS'

The 'Sun-grazer' Eros is an elongated asteroid. One of the most famous Sun-grazing asteroids is Icarus, which is named after the mythological character who flew too close to the Sun. Icarus is just 1.4 kilometres wide and comes to within 29 million kilometres of the Sun during its 1.1-year orbit. It actually glows red from the Sun's heat. In 1968, Icarus could be seen like a faint star travelling across the sky as it passed just 6.4 million kilometres from the Earth.

JUPITER

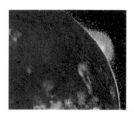

When the Solar System and the Sun were formed, Jupiter almost became another star. It is the largest planet, with a diameter of 142,800 kilometres. Jupiter is a huge ball of gases, including hydrogen, helium, ammonium, hydrogen sulphide and phosphorus. Bands of clouds of these gases swirl around Jupiter, which rotates quicker than any other planet – taking just 10 hours.

The colourful surface of Jupiter is dominated by the Great Red Spot, a swirling hurricane of gases where winds reach speeds of 350 kilometres per hour. The Great Red Spot measures 32,000 kilometres by 12,000 kilometres and could swallow up the Earth several times. Jupiter has at least 16 moons, and there could be many more that are too small to see. Its four major moons, from largest to smallest, are Ganymede, Callisto, Io and Europa. Jupiter also has a small ring system that cannot be seen from Earth. It was discovered by a spacecraft sent to explore the giant planet.

Galilean moon

JUPITER FACT FILE

Diameter: 142,800 km

Average distance from Sun: 778.3 million km

Length of a year: 11.9 Earth years

Number of moons: 16

*Faint rings made
of dust particles*

Great Red Spot

THE LARGEST PLANET

*Jupiter is the largest planet in the Solar System.
Astronomers believe that it is a failed star which, had
it been a bit bigger, could have helped to form a
double-star system. Galileo made the first recorded
observations of Jupiter through a telescope and saw four
small specks orbiting the planet. These moved position
each day. They are known as the Galilean moons.*

JUPITER'S MOONS

The surface of Io is a dramatic
world of orange, yellow and
white deposits of sulphur and
sulphur dioxide, with active
volcanoes. Europa is like a huge
ice pack, streaked with cracks.
Underneath the ice pack there
may be oceans of water, which
some scientists think could be
a source of basic living cells.
Ganymede, the largest of the
Galilean moons, has a surface
which looks like a badly cracked
eggshell, and Callisto has a
pockmarked surface that
resembles the skin of an
avocado pear.

51

SATURN

 Saturn is the second largest planet in the Solar System. It has a diameter of 119,300 kilometres. Saturn takes 29.5 Earth years to make a complete orbit of the Sun. It was not long before early astronomers began to realize that Saturn is the most beautiful planet in the Solar System because it has a spectacular ring system. Saturn's rings are made up of thousands of 'ringlets' of small bits of rock and ice, all held together in an orbit by the planet's gravity.

Saturn also has at least 23 moons and may have many more. Some moons are within the ring system and are called 'shepherd' moons, because they appear to help to keep the ring system in place. Saturn is like a smaller version of Jupiter, its atmosphere consisting mainly of hydrogen. Under the clouds, which rotate around the planet every 10 hours, are thick lakes of liquid hydrogen. The rocky core is 20,000 kilometres wide.

A SYSTEM OF RINGS
Saturn's ring system is made up of billions of 'snowballs' of rock and ice. They range in size from small flakes to chunks over 10 metres wide.

Brightest ring

TITANIC MOON

Saturn's largest and most famous moon is Titan, which has a diameter of 5,140 kilometres. Titan is the only moon in the Solar System with an atmosphere. Its thick atmosphere is made of nitrogen and methane gas. Titan may have lakes of liquid gas on its surface. Another of Saturn's moons is Mimas. It is smaller than Titan but has an enormous 130-km-wide crater on its surface. The crater looks like the giant eye of an alien.

_Outermost ring
visible from Earth_

RINGS OF COLOUR

Saturn's colourful rings do not actually touch the planet but are tilted at an angle to its orbit. The three main rings can be seen from Earth through a telescope – the outermost ring may be as much as 300,000 kilometres wide. Saturn's rings are not solid, and the light from bright stars shines straight through them.

URANUS

Uranus was the first planet to be 'discovered' – by English astronomer Sir William Herschel in 1781. It circles the Sun every 84 years at an average distance from the Sun of 2,867 million kilometres. The poles of this rather unusual planet point almost sideways, at an angle of 98 degrees. It is possible that Uranus was knocked over by a large body in the early history of the Solar System. Uranus is a bluish-green gas planet made up mainly of hydrogen and helium, with some methane. It has a very thin ring system of at least nine faint rings. The rings, which consist of rocks and dust, were only detected by astronomers in 1977. Uranus also has five large moons – Miranda, Ariel, Umbriel, Titania and Oberon – as well as 10 small moonlets.

WILLIAM HERSCHEL
Uranus was the first planet to be 'discovered' – by William Herschel using a telescope in 1781, in Bath, England. All the other planets closer to the Sun can be seen with the naked eye.

Diameter: 50,800 km

Average distance from Sun:
2,867 million km

Length of a year: 84 Earth years

Number of moons: 15

HERSCHEL'S DISCOVERY

Herschel made his discovery using a telescope in his garden in Bath, England. He compared the position of a star-like object in the night sky against a star map and noticed that, during the following days, the object appeared to move in relation to the stars. He had discovered the seventh planet. Earlier astronomers had seen Uranus but had not noticed its slight movement in the sky.

A BLUE-GREEN PLANET

The methane gas in the atmosphere of Uranus gives the planet its bluish-green colour. Methane gas accounts for about one-seventh of the atmosphere. Passing spacecraft found streaks of cloud in the planet's upper atmosphere. Astronomers know very little about the surface of Uranus.

NEPTUNE AND PLUTO

Neptune is a gaseous planet made of hydrogen and helium. It is very like Uranus but it is largely blue in colour due to the composition of its atmosphere. Neptune has a very active atmosphere with high-speed winds that swirl around the planet faster than it rotates. The winds carry 'scooter clouds' around the planet at speeds of 2,400 kilometres per hour. Neptune's orbit sometimes extends beyond the orbit of Pluto, and from 1979 to 1999 Neptune was farther away from the Sun than Pluto.

Neptune has two large moons, Triton and Nereid. Triton, one of the largest moons in the Solar System, is unusual because it moves in a circular orbit from east to west.

Pluto may well have been a moon of Neptune at one time. Its surface probably consists of frozen water, ammonia and methane. Pluto is the most distant planet from the Sun. It takes 248 years to orbit the Sun and won't return to the position it was discovered in until 2177! It was discovered in 1930 by an American astronomer, Clyde Tombaugh.

NEPTUNE FACT FILE

Diameter: 49,500 km

Average distance from Sun:
4,495 million km

Length of a year:
165 Earth years

Number of moons: 8

PLUTO FACT FILE

Diameter: 2,285 km

Average distance from Sun:
5,890 million km

Length of a year:
248 Earth years

Number of moons: 1

Astronomers predicted the existence of another planet beyond Uranus before it was finally discovered by a German, Johann Galle, in 1846. They had noticed that Uranus was not staying in a completely stable orbit around the Sun, and suspected that it was being pulled slightly off course by the gravity of another body. Mathematicians calculated where this possible planet might be, and Neptune was found in almost the exact spot predicted by Galle.

Pluto was discovered by Clyde Tombaugh after an extensive search which began at the Lowell Observatory, Arizona, USA. He compared photographic plates of the night sky and saw that a 'star' had moved.

THE DOUBLE PLANET

Temperatures on Pluto, the farthest planet from the Sun, are extremely low, ranging from about −230 degrees Celsius to −200 degrees Celsius. Pluto was the last planet to be discovered, and even the most powerful telescopes on Earth only show it as a star-like point of light. Pluto's moon, Charon, was discovered in 1978. It is almost the same size as Pluto, and the Pluto–Charon system is rather like a double planet. Charon circles Pluto every 6.3 days. Because Pluto rotates every 6.3 days, Charon appears to be stationary in the sky, like a geostationary satellite orbiting the Earth.

COMETS

Head of comet

Comets are also made from material left over when the Solar System was formed. They are like 'dirty snowballs' of rock, dust and ice. They travel in various orbits around the Sun, usually going deep into the far reaches of the Solar System. The orbits of some comets bring them close to the Sun after many years in darkness. When they come near to the Sun, comets reflect the Sun's light and can be seen in our sky. The Sun's heat and light also make comets shed material, which normally forms into the characteristic long tail.

One of the most famous comets is Halley's Comet, which appears in our skies every 74 years. When it last came close to the Sun, in 1986, it was rather a disappointing sight. Recently, a much more spectacular comet was Hale–Bopp. It shone brightly in the night skies in 1996–1997, and had a spectacular double tail.

COMET KOHOUTEK
Comets are named after the people who discovered them. Lubos Kohoutek found a comet in 1970. It was observed from space by the Skylab 4 crew in early 1974.

COMETS IN ORBIT

As a comet approaches the Sun, the heat makes it expand, evaporating gas and releasing dust. The gas and dust form a fuzzy head and a long tail. About 400 comets take between 3 and 200 years to orbit the Sun. There are about 500 known comets which will not return to the region around the Sun for thousands of years.

Tail of gas and dust

HALLEY'S COMET

The first recorded sighting of Halley's Comet was in 86 BC. The comet appeared again in 1066, at the time of the Battle of Hastings. It can be seen on the famous Bayeux Tapestry. After another appearance in 1301, the Italian artist Giotto di Bondone depicted it in his famous painting, *The Adoration of the Magi*. It was named after Edmond Halley who, in the early 18th century, realized that sightings in 1682, 1607 and 1531 must have been of the same comet. He therefore predicted its appearance in 1756, and the comet was named after him.

METEORITES

 Another kind of material left over from the formation of the Solar System consists of rocks of all shapes and sizes, and grain-like particles of dust. These are meteoroids. They enter Earth's atmosphere at speeds of up to 50 kilometres per second, burning up to leave behind a visible trail of hot gases called a meteor, or shooting star.

ARIZONA CRATER
An 80-metre-wide meteorite is thought to have hit the Earth in about 25,000 BC. It created a huge crater 1,265 metres wide and 175 metres deep in Canyon Diablo, near Winslow, Arizona, USA. The meteorite crashed with the force of a huge nuclear bomb.

Showers of meteors tend to occur during certain periods of the year. For example, the Earth encounters dust from Halley's Comet, which forms meteor showers in May and October. As these appear in the part of the sky where the constellations of Aquarius and Orion are at the time, they are called the Aquarids and the Orionids. Some of the larger rocks, which cause the occasional spectacular shooting star, survive the high-speed entry and reach the Earth. These are called meteorites. Several very large meteorites have hit the Earth in its history, forming craters that we can still see today.

METEORITE CLUES

About 500 meteorites hit the Earth each year. The largest known meteorite was found at Grootfontein in Namibia, southwest Africa, in 1920. It is 2.75 metres long and 2.43 metres wide and weighs 59 tonnes. Recovered meteorites provide scientists with an opportunity to study some of the oldest original material in the Solar System. Grains of dust from a meteorite that fell in Murchison, Victoria, Australia on 28 September 1969 are thought to be older than the Solar System itself.

Index

ACKNOWLEDGEMENTS

The publishers wish to thank the following artists who have
contributed to this book.

Julian Baker, Kuo Kang Chen, Rob Jakeway, Darrell Warner
(Beehive Illustrations) Guy Smith, Janos Marffy,
Peter Sarson.

Photographs supplied by Genesis Photo Library and
Miles Kelly Archive.